ALAN HUTCHISON PUBLISHING LTD

THE
WEDDING
BOOK

THE
ENGAGEMENT

The First Meeting

The Rivals
Sir William Orchardson. National Galleries of Scotland

The Engagement

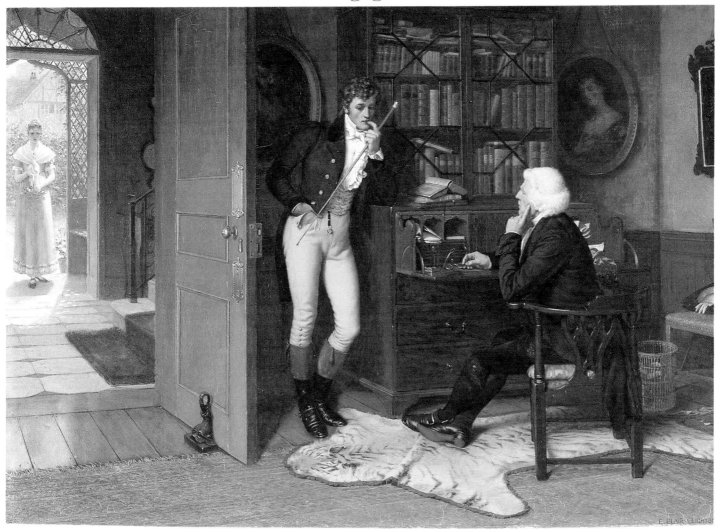

Date

Place

Time

Prospects
Edmund Leighton. Fine Art Photographs

The Occasion

The Ring

The Windmiller's Guest 1898
Edmund Blair Leighton. Fine Art Photographs

The Engagement Party

Invitation List

The Engagement Party

Invitation List

The Party

Love's Oracle

A. Ritzburger. Nottingham Castle Museum and Art Gallery

The Wedding Invitation

The Ceremony

Guest List

The Ceremony

Guest List

Bazille and Camille
Claude Monet. The National Gallery of Art, Washington. Ailsa Mellon Bruce Collection

The Reception

Guest List

The Reception

Guest List

The Reception

Guest List

The Reception

Guest List

The Lovers

The Reception

Guest List

The Swing
Pierre-Auguste Renoir. Musées Nationaux, France

The Reception

Guest List

Presents Received

Present

From

Thank you letter sent

Present

From

Thank you letter sent

Present

From

Thank you letter sent

Present

From

Thank you letter sent

Present

From

Thank you letter sent

Present

From

Thank you letter sent

Present

From

Thank you letter sent

Present

From

Thank you letter sent

Present

From

Thank you letter sent

Present

From

Thank you letter sent

Presents Received

Present

From

Thank you letter sent

Present

From

Thank you letter sent

Present

From

Thank you letter sent

Present

From

Thank you letter sent

Present

From

Thank you letter sent

Present

From

Thank you letter sent

Present

From

Thank you letter sent

Present

From

Thank you letter sent

Present

From

Thank you letter sent

Present

From

Thank you letter sent

Present

From

Thank you letter sent

Present

From

Thank you letter sent

Presents Received

Present

From

Thank you letter sent

Present

From

Thank you letter sent

Present

From

Thank you letter sent

Present

From

Thank you letter sent

Present

From

Thank you letter sent

Present

From

Thank you letter sent

Present

From

Thank you letter sent

Present

From

Thank you letter sent

Present

From

Thank you letter sent

Present

From

Thank you letter sent

Present

From

Thank you letter sent

Present

From

Thank you letter sent

Presents Received

Present

From

Thank you letter sent

Present

From

Thank you letter sent

Present

From

Thank you letter sent

Present

From

Thank you letter sent

Present

From

Thank you letter sent

Present

From

Thank you letter sent

Present

From

Thank you letter sent

Present

From

Thank you letter sent

Present

From

Thank you letter sent

Present

From

Thank you letter sent

Presents Received

Present	*Present*
From	*From*
Thank you letter sent	*Thank you letter sent*
Present	*Present*
From	*From*
Thank you letter sent	*Thank you letter sent*
Present	*Present*
From	*From*
Thank you letter sent	*Thank you letter sent*
Present	*Present*
From	*From*
Thank you letter sent	*Thank you letter sent*
Present	*Present*
From	*From*
Thank you letter sent	*Thank you letter sent*
Present	*Present*
From	*From*
Thank you letter sent	*Thank you letter sent*

Presents Received

Present	*Present*
From	*From*
Thank you letter sent	*Thank you letter sent*
Present	*Present*
From	*From*
Thank you letter sent	*Thank you letter sent*
Present	*Present*
From	*From*
Thank you letter sent	*Thank you letter sent*
Present	*Present*
From	*From*
Thank you letter sent	*Thank you letter sent*
Present	*Present*
From	*From*
Thank you letter sent	*Thank you letter sent*
Present	*Present*
From	*From*
Thank you letter sent	*Thank you letter sent*

Presents Received

Present

From

Thank you letter sent

Present

From

Thank you letter sent

Present

From

Thank you letter sent

Present

From

Thank you letter sent

Present

From

Thank you letter sent

Present

From

Thank you letter sent

Present

From

Thank you letter sent

Present

From

Thank you letter sent

Present

From

Thank you letter sent

Present

From

Thank you letter sent

Present

From

Thank you letter sent

Present

From

Thank you letter sent

Presents Received

Present

From

Thank you letter sent

Present

From

Thank you letter sent

Present

From

Thank you letter sent

Present

From

Thank you letter sent

Present

From

Thank you letter sent

Present

From

Thank you letter sent

Present

From

Thank you letter sent

Present

From

Thank you letter sent

Present

From

Thank you letter sent

Present

From

Thank you letter sent

THE WEDDING DAY PREPARATIONS

◆

The Order of the Day

The Bride's Dress

The Seamstress
C. Baugniet. Bridgeman Art Library

The Bride's Dress

Wedding Morning
John Henry Frederick Bacon. National Museums and Galleries on Merseyside

The Bridesmaids' Dresses

The Bridesmaid
James Tissot. Collection of the Leeds Art Gallery

The Bride's Headdress

The Bridesmaids' Headdresses

The Bride's Mother's Outfit

The Bride's Family

Still Life with a Garland of Flowers
Jan Brueghel. Musées Royaux des Beaux Arts de Belgique

Flowers, Bouquets and Buttonholes

THE
CEREMONY

◆

The Journey to the Wedding

Pimlico
Walter Sickert. Aberdeen Art Gallery and Museums

Arrivals

The Groom and the Best Man

Arrivals

The Groom and the Best Man

The Bride

The Bridesmaids and Pages

Arrivals

The Bridesmaids and Pages

Arrivals

The Maids of Honour and the Ushers

Arrivals

The Families

Arrivals

The Families

The Order of Service

The Service

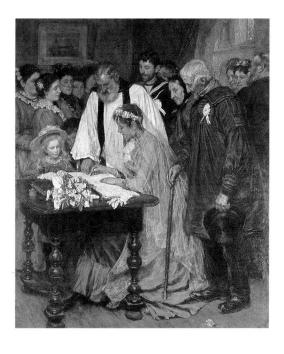

Signing the Marriage Register
James Charles, Bradford City Art Gallery and Museum. Bridgeman Art Library

The Wedding Reception

G. E. Hicks. Fine Art Photographs

After the Ceremony

After the Ceremony

Journey to the Reception

The Village Wedding
Luke Fildes. Private Collection. The Bridgeman Art Library

THE RECEPTION

The Place

The Time

Decorations and Flowers

The Wedding Meal
Albert-Auguste Fourie. Musées des Beaux-Arts, Rouen. Lauros-Giraudon – Bridgeman Art Library

The Speeches

The Speeches

The Cake

The Food and Drink

The Health of the Bride
Stanhope Forbes. The Tate Gallery

The Food and Drink

XLIII.

OW do I love thee? Let me count
    the ways.
    I love thee to the depth and
      breadth and height
    My soul can reach, when feeling
      out of sight
    For the ends of Being and ideal
      Grace.
I love thee to the level of every day's
Most quiet need, by sun and candle-light.
I love thee freely, as men strive for Right;
I love thee purely, as they turn from Praise.
I love thee with the passion put to use
In my old griefs, and with my childhood's faith,
I love thee with a love I seemed to lose
With my lost saints, — I love thee with the breath,
Smiles, tears, of all my life! — and, if God choose,
I shall but love thee better after death.

XLIX

Decoration to Sonnets from the Portuguese by Elizabeth Barrett Browning
Adrian J. Lorio. Victoria and Albert Museum

Telegrams and Messages

Embroidery by Mrs. George Jack of The Rose Garden by Dante Gabriel Rossetti
Victoria and Albert Museum

Telegrams and Messages

Dance in the Town
Pierre-Auguste Renoir. Musées Nationaux, France

Entertainments and Music

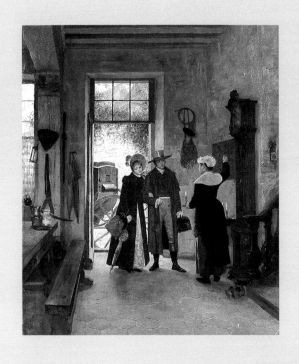

THE
HONEYMOON

Going Away Clothes

The Marriage of Giovanni Arnolfini and Giovanna Cenami
Jan van Eyck. The National Gallery

The Honeymoon Wardrobe

Going Away

Going Away

Going Away

Going Away

In Love
Marcus Stone. Nottingham Castle Museum and Art Gallery

The Journey

The Final Destination

The Honeymoon

Pleading
Sir Lawrence Alma-Tadema. Bridgeman Art Library

The Honeymoon

The Honeymoon

Detail of a Marriage Quilt
English. 1829 Victoria and Albert Museum

MEMORIES

The Bride's Memories

A Passing Cloud
Marcus Stone. Manchester City Art Gallery

The Bride's Memories

The Bride's Memories

The Groom's Memories

The Morning Walk
Thomas Gainsborough. The National Gallery

The Groom's Memories

Picking Flowers
Pierre-Auguste Renoir. The National Gallery of Art, Washington. Ailsa Mellon Bruce Collection

The Groom's Memories

Hopes for the Future

King René's Honeymoon
Ford Madox Brown. The National Museum of Wales

Published by Alan Hutchison Publishing Company,
9 Pembridge Studios, 27A Pembridge Villas, London W11 3EP

Worldwide Distribution

Printed and bound in Hong Kong
Designed by Guy Callaby
© Alan Hutchison Publishing Company
ISBN 1 85272 935 X

Cover:
Signing the Register (detail)
Edmund Blair Leighton. City of Bristol Museum and Art Gallery. Bridgeman Art Library

Frontispiece:
The Wedding Morn
Richard Redgrave. Victoria and Albert Museum

Back Cover:
On the Threshold
Edmund Blair Leighton. Manchester City Art Gallery

Title Pages:
THE ENGAGEMENT
The Garden of Eden
Hugh Riviere. Bridgeman Art Library

THE WEDDING DAY PREPARATIONS
Her Wedding Day
Anton Weiss. Bridgeman Art Library

THE CEREMONY
Signing the Register
Edmund Blair Leighton. City of Bristol Museum and Art Gallery
Bridgeman Art Library

THE RECEPTION
A Wedding Toast
Erik Henningsen, Britta Jacobsen. The Bridgeman Art Library

THE HONEYMOON
The Arrival at the Inn
Charles Edward Delart. Phillips Fine Art Auctioneers

MEMORIES
The Lovers' Tryst
Richard Redgrave. Fine Art Photographs